Pennsylvania Railroad Company

Tour to California

Pennsylvania Railroad Company

Tour to California

ISBN/EAN: 9783337194765

Printed in Europe, USA, Canada, Australia, Japan

Cover: Foto ©Andreas Hilbeck / pixelio.de

More available books at **www.hansebooks.com**

TOUR

TO

CALIFORNIA,

BY THE

"GOLDEN GATE SPECIAL,"

UNDER THE PERSONALLY-CONDUCTED TOURIST SYSTEM

OF THE

PENNSYLVANIA RAILROAD.

———— —◄●►———— —

PASSENGER DEPARTMENT.

1899.

J. R. WOOD,
Gen'l Passenger Agent.

GEO. W. BOYD,
Asst. Gen'l Passenger Agent.

PENNSYLVANIA RAILROAD

PERSONALLY-CONDUCTED TOUR

THROUGH

CALIFORNIA.

◄••►

THE Personally-Conducted Tour through California laid out in the following pages has
been arranged for the special benefit of
those who desire to visit the points of
interest in this "Paradise of the Pacific"
and enjoy its matchless climate in a
thoroughly satisfactory manner, at a
minimum expense, and with the least
loss of time. Arrangements have there-
fore been made to use the "Golden
Gate Special," the finest train that has ever crossed the
continent, over the entire route, leaving it only at those
points where magnificent hotels of world-wide fame offer
attractions equal to those of the special train. This arrangement places the palatial train at the disposal of the

tourists at all times, and it is the first California tour ever projected which included this important feature. The train will be run on a special schedule adapted to the particular needs of the tourists. The advantages of these original features are readily apparent, as they enable tourists to cover as much territory as they could in twice the time by regular trains, besides enjoying the luxurious accommodations which the special train affords. Stops will be made at all desirable points *en route* and ample time allotted for their satisfactory inspection. The schedule is so arranged that the picturesque points along the line will be passed by daylight.

Previous experience with tours through California has shown that during the height of the season it is difficult, at some of the most attractive points, to secure satisfactory accommodations at hotels, owing to their crowded condition. By having the special train in service at all times through California, the tourists are rendered entirely independent in this respect.

The party will be under the guidance of an experienced Tourist Agent, who will have entire charge of the special train throughout. He will be assisted by an accomplished Chaperon, whose particular charge will be the unescorted ladies of the party.

For those desiring to use the "Golden Gate Special" going, and travel independently through California, special rates will be found on page 24.

The tour will cover a period of thirty-five days, nineteen of which will be spent in California. Stops will be made at Mammoth Cave, Montgomery, Mobile, New Orleans, during Mardi Gras festivities; San Antonio, El Paso, Los Angeles, San Diego, Riverside, Redlands, Pasadena, Santa Barbara, Monterey, Santa Cruz, San José, Mount Hamilton and Lick Observatory, Menlo Park and Stanford University, San Francisco, Salt Lake City, Glenwood Springs, Royal

Gorge, Colorado Springs, Manitou and Garden of the Gods, Denver, and Chicago.

The coupons for the side trips to Mammoth Cave, San Diego, Redlands, Santa Barbara, Mount Hamilton, and Monterey may be used or not, at the pleasure of the holder; if they remain entirely unused they will be redeemed at the General Office of the Pennsylvania Railroad Company, Philadelphia, in accordance with the usual rules governing the redemption of tickets. In case it is desired to visit other resorts in California, not included in the side trips, excursion tickets will be sold by the local railroads.

The headquarters of the Tourist Agent and Chaperon, on the Pacific Coast, is 20 Montgomery Street, San Francisco. Members of the parties, whose movements in California are not fixed in advance, may have their letters or telegrams sent there in care of the Tourist Agent, whence they will be forwarded to the tourist's temporary address. In order to insure prompt forwarding of mail, such tourists should keep our San Francisco office fully advised as to their movements while on the Pacific Coast. Mail designed to reach tourists while *en route* should be forwarded "In care of Tourist Agent Pennsylvania Railroad Tour," at the hotels used by the tour as outlined in itinerary.

Complete details of the tour will be developed in the following pages.

THE "GOLDEN GATE SPECIAL."

The special train used by the party over the entire route will consist of a Pullman Composite Smoking Car, a Dining Car, Compartment Car, Drawing-room Sleeping Cars, and an Observation Car. The train will be an exact counterpart of the world-renowned PENNSYLVANIA LIMITED, which, by universal verdict, is the handsomest and best-appointed passenger train in existence.

A brief sketch of the cars in the order in which the train is made up will serve to give a faint conception of its magnificence.

The Pullman Vestibule Composite Car is exclusively a gentleman's car. The forward end is set apart for baggage. A compartment introduced in this car is fitted up as a barber shop and bath room. A regular barber's chair and all the paraphernalia of the tonsorial artist are at hand. A bath tub with hot and cold water occupies one side of the compartment. Adjoining the bath room is a refreshment compartment, from which exhilarating beverages may be secured in response to the tap of an electric bell.

The main portion of the car is a smoking saloon. It is finished in natural wood, furnished with comfortable rattan arm chairs, a lounge, a sofa, and two writing desks, each surmounted by a small case of selected books. This car will supply all the comfort of one's club, and cannot fail to receive the indorsement of masculine appreciation.

In this as in the other cars of the train, handsome chandeliers of nickel or brass depend from the roof, fitted with gas burners and electric-light bulbs. Apart from the stationary lights there are also movable electric lights attached by insulated wire to the sides of the car, capable of being shifted to any position desired by the user. This admirable arrangement originated with, and was introduced into practical use by, the electrical department of Pullman's Palace Car Company.

The Dining Car is not only a dining room in which forty people, disposed at ten tables, can dine in the most comfortable manner, but it contains a kitchen in which four cooks can prepare meals for twice the seating capacity of the car, a storage room for the provisions, ice chests for wines, china closets, linen lockers, and the entire outfit of a large restaurant.

A conspicuous advantage of the Dining Car, and one that

DINING CAR, "GOLDEN GATE SPECIAL."

is appreciated most highly by all long-distance travelers, is the regularity with which meals are served, and the liberal time allowed for taking them.

The hours for meals will be observed as follows:—

Breakfast	7.00 to 9.30 A. M.
Luncheon	12.30 to 2.00 P. M.
Dinner	6.00 to 7.30 P. M.

LUXURIOUS SLEEPING CARS.

The Pullman Vestibule Sleeping Cars composing this train are the best examples of nineteenth century car building. The Compartment Car is one of Pullman's latest inventions. It contains ten state rooms, all handsomely furnished and equipped with every convenience of a private boudoir. These compartments may be made communicating or rendered absolutely exclusive, as desired. The Sleeping Cars each contain ten sections of two double berths, a drawing room, and two state rooms. The drawing room and state room can be made communicating. Toilet rooms for ladies and gentlemen occupy separate ends of the car. The drawing rooms are equipped with lavatories and private toilet annexes. The state rooms have washstands and toilet. In addition to the chandeliers, movable lights are attached to each section, so that one may lie in one's berth and read, with the light disposed as best suited to the reader's convenience.

A maid is in attendance, ready to serve the ladies, and always on the alert to anticipate their wants.

THE OBSERVATION CAR.

By large odds the most popular car in the train, and one which exemplifies the latest development of transcontinental travel, is the Observation Car, which brings up the rear. Its interior presents a revelation in car construction. The body of the car is an open sitting room, finished in hard wood, and furnished with rattan arm chairs and sofas. Among its conveniences are a writing desk, a library of selected books, movable tables, and a piano. The daylight streams through handsome plate-glass windows,

OBSERVATION CAR, "GOLDEN GATE SPECIAL."

and at night the incandescent lights, both from the overhead electroliers and the movable globes, serve to thoroughly illuminate the interior. The rear door is composed of plate glass from its top to within two feet of the floor. The rear platform is deeply recessed, so as to form an open observatory. The protecting sides of the car and the overhanging roof shelter its occupants while they sit and enjoy an unobstructed view of the scenery. The platform will accommodate about twenty people in camp chairs. This car is for the free use of every passenger.

The entire train will be heated by steam and lighted by electricity generated by the dynamo or drawn from the storage batteries.

HINTS ON CLOTHING.

Light and heavy changes of underwear will be needed. If one would follow the customs of the country, woolen clothing should be worn, as the natives of California wear woolen garments of the same weight throughout the year. Overcoats, shawls, or convenient wraps should be carried, and rubber shoes and gossamers may at any time be called into requisition.

Ladies fond of horseback and bicycle riding should by all means take their habits, as many opportunities will present themselves for charming rides.

BAGGAGE.

One hundred and fifty pounds of baggage are allowed on each whole ticket and seventy-five pounds on each half ticket ; all in excess of these amounts will be charged for at usual excess baggage rates ; one may carry every essential garment in a moderate-sized trunk.

Tourists should procure, at time tickets are purchased, special baggage tags, on which name and home address should be plainly written, and one of these tags attached to each piece of baggage to be checked, to serve as a ready means of identification. Baggage to be used on the

"Golden Gate Special" on the going trip should be tagged, and checked through to Los Angeles.

The checks representing baggage desired *en route* will be collected on the train by special baggage master of the Pennsylvania Railroad Company, who will attend to all necessary transfer and delivery to rooms at hotels, and who will also deliver to passengers, prior to arrival at final destination of train, claim checks to enable them to secure this baggage at the conclusion of the trip. Any small satchels containing necessary articles for use on train *en route* can be readily accommodated in sleepers or in the baggage compartment of the Composite Car, where access can be had at the convenience of the owner.

Baggage not required until arrival on the Pacific Coast should be checked to Los Angeles by regular trains. A similar method should be observed in checking baggage on the homeward journey.

ITINERARY.

•

Besides berth in sleeping car and all the extra conveniences on the "Golden Gate Special," the rates for this tour include transportation, meals, transfers, hotel accommodations, carriage drives, and other features as outlined in the following itinerary. (See page 24.)

WEDNESDAY, FEBRUARY 8.

Leave Boston in Pullman sleeping car, attached to the Boston and Philadelphia night express, via New York, New Haven and Hartford Railroad (Park Square Station), 7.00 P. M., Providence 8.17 P. M., New London 10.15 P. M., New Haven 11.50 P. M.; arrive at Philadelphia 6.40 A. M. following day. Breakfast in the Broad Street Station restaurant. Remain in Philadelphia until 10.25 A. M., when the special train leaves that city.

THURSDAY, FEBRUARY 9.

Leave New York, Pennsylvania Railroad Stations, West Twenty-third Street at 7.50 A. M., foot of Courtlandt and Desbrosses Streets, by special train (described elsewhere), at 8.00 A. M. (Brooklyn, via annex boat, at 7.33 A. M.), Jersey City 8.13 A. M., Newark 8.28 A. M., and Trenton 9.28 A. M. Leave Philadelphia at 10.25 A. M., where the New England party will join the special train. Leave Harrisburg 1.00 P. M., arrive at Pittsburg 7.10 P. M. Leave Pittsburg 6.30 P. M. Central time. Luncheon and dinner in the dining car. Eastern time becomes Central time at Pittsburg, and watches should be set back one hour.

FRIDAY, FEBRUARY 10.

Arrive at Cincinnati, the "Queen City," over the Pennsylvania Lines at 5.40 A. M. Leave Cincinnati, via the Louisville and Nashville Railroad, at 6.00 A. M. Arrive at Glasgow Junction 12.30 P. M., and leave at 12.40 P. M. for Mammoth Cave. After tour of this great natural wonder tourists will leave at 5.30 P. M. for Glasgow Junction, which will be reached at 6.15 and left at 6.25 P. M., via Louisville and Nashville Railroad, for Montgomery, Ala. Breakfast, luncheon, and dinner in dining car.

SATURDAY, FEBRUARY 11.

Arrive Montgomery at 7.00 A. M., where a stop of four hours will be made. Leave at 11.00 A. M., reach Mobile at 4.00 P. M., and have three hours here before leaving at 7.00 P. M., via Louisville and Nashville Railroad, for New Orleans, which is reached at midnight. Breakfast, luncheon, and dinner in dining car.

SUNDAY, FEBRUARY 12,
MONDAY, FEBRUARY 13,
TUESDAY, FEBRUARY 14.

In New Orleans. Visit points of interest and view Mardi Gras festivities, for which seat will be provided. The special train will be located on Clairbourne Street for occupancy, and will be the home of the tourists during the entire stay in the "Crescent City." All meals in dining car.

WEDNESDAY, FEBRUARY 15.

Leave New Orleans at 3.00 A. M. via Southern Pacific Company (Atlantic System). Breakfast, luncheon, and dinner in dining car.

THURSDAY, FEBRUARY 16.

Arrive San Antonio 6.00 A. M. Four hours for sightseeing, which will be fully occupied, as there are many points of historic interest which may be reached by electric cars. Leave San Antonio 10.00 A. M. Breakfast, luncheon, and dinner in dining car.

FRIDAY, FEBRUARY 17.

Arrive at El Paso at 8.00 A. M. Central time, or 6.00 A. M. Pacific time. Remain at El Paso six hours. The quaintness of El Paso, with its picturesque situation, is strongly marked. Across the river, connected by horse cars, lies the old town of Paso del Norte, newly named Juarez, both places, with their crooked streets, irregular roads, and sunburnt brick houses, speaking eloquently of the Mexican. At El Paso Central time changes to Pacific, and watches should be set back two hours. Leave El Paso 12.00 noon, Pacific time. Breakfast, luncheon, and dinner in dining car.

SATURDAY, FEBRUARY 18.

On the Southern Pacific Railroad, in Arizona and Southern California. The vast Western plains traversed from El Paso unfold the cramped ideas many Eastern minds have of the reported wonderfully extensive, and as yet unoccupied, territory of this section of the States. It is hard to realize that for hours, and as far as the eye can penetrate on either side of the tracks, lie the richest of lands. Mile after mile of it, absolutely uninhabited, is left behind in the train's onward flight. Through New Mexico and Arizona is witnessed and enjoyed a phenomenally clear atmosphere and a cloudless, sunlit sky. In this latter Territory, near Yuma, in the bed of a once deep lake, can be discerned the most marvelous mirage. For miles the train seems to run along the margin of a chain of lakes, here and there tiny islets fringed with trees seem to dot the waters, and the shadows of mountains and hills are reflected on what appears to be a mirror of clear water.

All through this section of Arizona are to be found the mounds and hieroglyphics of the cliff dwellers. Sixty-five miles west of Tucson are the ruins of Casa Grande, once seven stories high, and antedating probably the Christian era. On the south side of the Salt River may be seen the ruins of a vast canal, one hundred and twenty miles long, irrigating sixteen hundred square miles, the work of these prehistoric people. Breakfast and luncheon in dining car. At 4.00 P. M. Los Angeles will be reached. Tourists will be transferred to the Van Nuys Hotel, where accommodations will be provided during the stay in Los Angeles.

SUNDAY, FEBRUARY 19.
MONDAY, FEBRUARY 20.

In Los Angeles. Independent side trips can be made by the tourists to the numerous points of interest in the vicinity of Los Angeles; such as Santa Catalina Island, Santa Monica, and Lucky Baldwin's Ranch.

MONDAY, FEBRUARY 20.

The "Golden Gate Special" will be placed for occupancy during the evening, and Los Angeles will be left after midnight.

TUESDAY, FEBRUARY 21.

Breakfast in dining car. Arrive San Diego 8.00 A. M., when passengers and baggage will be transferred to the Hotel del Coronado, where accommodations will be provided.

WEDNESDAY, FEBRUARY 22.

Retire in train after 9.00 P. M., and leave during the night for Riverside.

THURSDAY, FEBRUARY 23.

Breakfast in dining car. Arrive at Riverside at 8.00 A. M. Carriage drive through the famous Magnolia Avenue. Leave at 12.00 noon. Luncheon in dining car.

Arrive Redlands 1.00 P. M. Carriage drive to Smiley Heights. Leave at 6.00 P. M. Dinner in dining car, and arrive at Pasadena at 9.00 P. M.

FRIDAY, FEBRUARY 24.
SATURDAY, FEBRUARY 25.

During the stay in Pasadena the "Golden Gate Special" will be sidetracked for occupancy, and all meals will be served in the dining car. Carriage drive in Pasadena is included in the ticket. Independent trips may be made to points of interest, including the Mt. Lowe Railway.

SATURDAY, FEBRUARY 25.

Leave Los Angeles at 6.00 P. M. Dinner in dining car. Arrive Los Angeles at 6.30 P. M., and leave via Southern Pacific Company's line at 7.00 P. M. Arrive Santa Barbara at midnight.

SUNDAY, FEBRUARY 26.
MONDAY, FEBRUARY 27.

In Santa Barbara. Carriage drive. All meals will be furnished in dining car.

MONDAY, FEBRUARY 27.

Leave Santa Barbara at 11.00 A. M. Tehachapi Pass will be reached at 5.00 P. M. Breakfast, luncheon, and dinner in dining car.

TUESDAY, FEBRUARY 28.

Arrive Del Monte at 8.00 A. M. Breakfast in dining car. Locate at the Hotel Del Monte. Carriage drive will be provided through the park.

WEDNESDAY, MARCH 1.

Retire on the special train during the evening, and leave after midnight for Santa Cruz.

THURSDAY, MARCH 2.

Arrive Santa Cruz at 7.00 A. M. Breakfast in dining car. Carriage drive. Passengers desiring to visit the Big Trees can use regular train leaving Santa Cruz by the Narrow Gauge Line during the afternoon, and rejoin the main party on the Golden Gate Special at San José. Leave Santa Cruz at 3.00 P. M. and arrive at San José at 6.00 P. M. Luncheon and dinner in dining car.

FRIDAY, MARCH 3.

Breakfast and luncheon in dining car. Trip to Mount Hamilton and the Lick Observatory, for which coupon will be included in the ticket. Luncheon *en route*. Retire on special train in the evening.

SATURDAY, MARCH 4.

Arrive at Menlo Park early in the morning. Breakfast in dining car, and carriage drive to the Leland Stanford, Jr., University and other points of interest. Leave at 12.00 noon. Luncheon in dining car. Arrive San Francisco at 1.00 P. M. Transfer to the Palace Hotel, where the party will be located during the stay in San Francisco.

SATURDAY, MARCH 4,
SUNDAY, MARCH 5,
MONDAY, MARCH 6,
TUESDAY, MARCH 7.

In San Francisco. Visit points of interest.

RETURNING.

.

TUESDAY, MARCH 7.

The party will take one of the handsome double-decked ferryboats at the Southern Pacific wharf, foot of Market Street, at 10.00 P. M., for Oakland, where their special train will be located in the station of the Southern Pacific Company. From Oakland the train passes over the Central Division of the Southern Pacific Company.

WEDNESDAY, MARCH 8.

The ascent of the Sierras will begin early in the morning, and the forenoon will be spent in the midst of the wild scenery of Cape Horn, Gold Run, Blue Cañon, and Emigrant Gap. Breakfast, luncheon, and dinner in dining car.

THURSDAY, MARCH 9.

Ogden will be reached early in the morning. At this point the standard of time changes to Mountain, one hour faster. Leave Ogden via Rio Grande Western Railway. After an hour's run Salt Lake City is reached.

After breakfast in the dining car the party will take a carriage drive through the city. Luncheon and dinner in dining car.

Leave Salt Lake City at 6.00 P. M. over the Rio Grande Western Railway.

FRIDAY, MARCH 10.

At Grand Junction, reached at 3.30 A. M., the train passes from the line of the Rio Grande Western Railway to that of the Denver and Rio Grande Railroad, and continues on its way to Glenwood Springs, reached at 6.30 A.M. At Glenwood Springs two hours will be allowed for visits to Springs, Bathing Pool, and other points of interest. Leave Glenwood Springs at 8.30 A.M. Soon after leaving Glenwood Springs the route traverses the Cañon of the Grand River and Eagle River Cañon. At 12.00 noon Tennessee Pass is reached, ten thousand four hundred and eighteen feet above sea level. Arrive at Leadville at 12.35 P. M., and Salida 2.50 P. M.

The journey will be continued from Salida through the Royal Gorge and the Grand Cañon of the Arkansas River, by Cañon City and Pueblo, to Colorado Springs, which will be reached at 11.00 P. M. The Royal Gorge and the Grand Cañon of the Arkansas are together about ten miles in length, beginning at Parkdale and ending at Cañon City. Breakfast, luncheon, and dinner in dining car.

SATURDAY, MARCH 11.

At Colorado Springs. Ample opportunity is afforded to see thoroughly this charming city under the shadow of Pike's Peak. A carriage ride through the " Garden of the Gods " and to Manitou is covered by ticket. Retire on train in the evening (sleepers open at 9.00 P. M.), and leave Colorado Springs at 11.00 P. M. for Denver via Denver and Rio Grande Railroad. Breakfast, luncheon, and dinner in dining car.

SUNDAY, MARCH 12.

The party will awaken in Denver, and Sunday will be spent in the city. Breakfast in dining car and carriage drive through the city. The party will be located at the magnificent Brown Palace Hotel, where luncheon and dinner will be served. Leave Denver by the Burlington Route at midnight. Cars will be open for occupancy at 9.00 P. M.

MONDAY, MARCH 13.

At McCook, Neb., reached at 7.30 A. M., Mountain time, the standard of time, changes to Central time, one hour faster.

During the day the party will pass through Nebraska, Hastings at 1.00 P. M., Lincoln at 4.00 P. M., and Pacific Junction at 6.10 P. M. Breakfast, luncheon, and dinner in dining car.

TUESDAY, MARCH 14.

Arrive in Chicago at 8.25 A. M. Breakfast in dining car. Carriage drive terminating at the Auditorium Hotel, where tourists will be located during the stay. Leave Chicago at 5.40 P. M. on the Pennsylvania Lines through Indiana and Ohio. Dinner in dining car.

WEDNESDAY, MARCH 15.

Over the main line of the Pennsylvania Railroad, along the Conemaugh Valley through the celebrated scenery of the Allegheny Mountains, around the Horse Shoe Curve, and through the Juniata Valley. Eastern time east of Pittsburg, one hour faster than Central time.

Arrive in Harrisburg 1.35 P. M., Philadelphia 4.17 P. M., Newark 6.07 P. M., and New York 6.30 P. M. Breakfast and luncheon in dining car. The New England tourists will take supper at Broad Street Station restaurant and use the Boston Express from Philadelphia 7.50 P. M., arriving in Boston early the next morning.

Round-Trip Rate from Boston $405 00

Round-Trip Rate from New York and
Philadelphia $400 00

Round-Trip Rate from Pittsburg . . $395 00

ROUND TRIP RATES FOR EXTRA PULLMAN ACCOMMODATIONS ON THE SPECIAL TRAIN.

PULLMAN ACCOMMODATIONS.	From New York and Philada.	From Pittsburg.
Double Pullman berth, one person	$400 00	$395 00
Section, one person	475 00	470 00
State room, two persons, each	435 00	430 00
Drawing room, two persons, each	470 00	465 00
Drawing room, three persons, each	425 00	420 00

The New York and Philadelphia rates will apply from points on the Pennsylvania Railroad system east of Pittsburg and north of and including Quantico, with proportionate rates from points west of Pittsburg on the Pennsylvania Company's Lines.

The special train will stop only at the principal stations on the Pennsylvania Railroad system ; but the price of the tickets covers the transportation in both directions of tourists who may start from other points at which tickets are sold to the nearest stations where connection may be made with the special train.

Tickets will be sold for children between the age of five and twelve years from Boston at $325.00, from New York, Philadelphia, and Pittsburg at $320.00, if separate Pullman accommodations are required ; or from Boston at $250.00, from New York, Philadelphia, and Pittsburg at $245.00, if they share the berths of parents or traveling companions.

The rates include railroad transportation; Pullman accommodations as per table given above, both *en route* and through California; meals in dining car on special train; transfer of person and baggage between the special train and hotels where stop is made over night; side trips to Riverside, San Bernardino, Redlands, Pasadena, Los Angeles, Santa Barbara, San Francisco, Monterey (Del Monte), Santa Cruz, Big Trees, San José, Mount Hamilton (Lick Observatory), and Menlo Park; admission to and guide in Mammoth Cave; a seat for the Mardi Gras festivities at New Orleans; transfer of passenger and baggage and hotel accommodations at Los Angeles; transfer at San Diego and accommodations at Del Coronado Hotel; carriage drives at Riverside, Redlands, Pasadena, Santa Barbara, Del Monte, Santa Cruz, and Menlo Park; transfer and accommodations at Hotel del Monte and carriage drive through park; transfers at San Francisco and accommodations at Palace Hotel; carriage ride Salt Lake City; carriage ride to Manitou and Garden of the Gods, Colorado Springs; carriage drive and luncheon and dinner (Brown Palace) Denver; carriage drive, transfer, and luncheon (The Auditorium) Chicago. In addition to the above, the tickets from Boston include sleeping-car accommodations (one berth) Boston to Philadelphia and return, breakfast going and supper returning at Broad Street Station, Philadelphia.

If side trips are not desired to San Diego, Riverside, Redlands, Pasadena, Santa Barbara, Del Monte, Santa Cruz, Mount Hamilton, and Menlo Park, and passengers travel independently on regular trains through California, from arrival at Los Angeles until departure from San Francisco, the rate will be $310.00 from New York; with side trips, $325.00.

A limited number of berths will be sold, using the " Golden Gate Special " in either direction, and regular trains in the other, in connection with regular Pacific

Coast excursion tickets, good for nine months and choice
of routes. Specific rates will be quoted upon application.

DISTANCE TABLE.

	MILES.
New York to Cincinnati	757
Cincinnati to Mammoth Cave	210
Mammoth Cave to New Orleans	729
New Orleans to El Paso	1,186
El Paso to Los Angeles	812
Los Angeles to San Diego	127
San Diego to Riverside	133
Riverside to Redlands	18
Redlands to Pasadena	59
Pasadena to Los Angeles	10
Los Angeles to Santa Barbara	110
Santa Barbara to Del Monte	589
Del Monte to Santa Cruz	47
Santa Cruz to San José	70
San José to top of Mount Hamilton and return	52
San José to San Francisco	50
San Francisco to Salt Lake City	871
Salt Lake City to Glenwood Springs	380
Glenwood Springs to Colorado Springs	292
Colorado Springs to Denver	75
Denver to Chicago	1,020
Chicago to New York	912
Total distance covered by ticket	8,509

NOTE.—The special train traverses seventeen States and
two Territories, as shown. *States:* New Jersey, Pennsyl-
vania, Ohio, Kentucky, Tennessee, Alabama, Mississippi,
Louisiana, Texas, California, Nevada, Utah, Colorado,
Nebraska, Iowa, Illinois, and Indiana. *Territories:* New
Mexico and Arizona.

WONDERFUL OBJECT LESSONS.

The following descriptive notes are intended to point out, in brief, the distinctive characteristics of points *en route* and in California. The impossibility of presenting an exhaustive description of the large number of resorts is manifest, as it would require a volume much too bulky for use as a guide book.

What has been written will serve as a finger board to point the way.

The trip as outlined is unquestionably the most desirable tour an American could take. Apart from the rare pleasure of visiting new places and of witnessing novel scenes, the tour will prove a better educator than any number of lectures heard or books on travel read. The immense scope of territory traversed will expand the ideas of all tourists, indelibly impress upon their minds enlarged views of this mighty Union and its vast possessions, and they will return to their homes prouder than ever of the great land whose borders are protected by the Stars and Stripes.

REDEMPTION OF TICKETS.

All tickets should be paid for at least one week prior to the date of departure of the tour.

If, for any reason, purchasers of tickets are unable to use them, the tickets will be redeemed, provided they are presented for redemption, either personally or by letter, at the General Office of the Company, Philadelphia, two days prior to the date of the tour. If tickets are partially used, the unused coupons will be redeemed under the usual rules of the various lines in interest.

Letters and requests for reservations of space or tickets may be addressed to Geo. W. Boyd, Assistant General Passenger Agent, Philadelphia, Pa., or to Tourist Agent, Pennsylvania Railroad, at the offices given below.

OFFICES OF TOURIST AGENTS OF THE COMPANY.

BOSTON . . . . 205 Washington Street.
NEW YORK . . . . 1196 Broadway.
BROOKLYN . . . . 860 Fulton Street.
NEWARK, N. J. . . . . 789 Broad Street.
PHILADELPHIA . . . . . Room 411, Broad Street Station.
BALTIMORE . . . . Baltimore and Calvert Streets.
WASHINGTON . . . . Fifteenth and G Streets.
PITTSBURG . . . . . . Fifth Avenue and Smithfield Street.

THE STAFF OF THE TOURIST BUREAU.

R. J. DE LONG, in charge.

Tourist Agents.	*Chaperons.*
W. N. BURCHARD,	MISS E. C. BINGHAM,
D. N. BELL,	MISS Z. W. BEATY,
C. R. ROSENBERG,	MISS A. E. BRADY.
J. S. MURPHY, JR.,	
H. Y. DARNELL.	

☞ The importance of reserving space at once is apparent, as the tour is absolutely limited not to exceed seventy-five persons.

DESCRIPTIVE OUTLINE SKETCHES

OF

INTERESTING POINTS *EN ROUTE* AND IN CALIFORNIA.

◄●►

MAMMOTH CAVE, KY.

967 miles from New York.

This cave, in which a distance of two hundred miles may be covered in following the numerous natural twists and turns, is undoubtedly one of the most interesting in the world, outrivaling even the one of Adelsberg in Austria. It is filled with grottoes, labyrinths, abysses, weird carved echoing chambers, streams, cascades, and lakes. The temperature in the cave is almost equal all the year. The entrance to the cave proper is very picturesque, leading down a steep rocky gorge. The tourist will pass through the Rotunda, along Audubon's Avenue, view the Little Bat Room, the Giant's Coffin, the Star Chamber, the Fairy Grotto, the Echo River, and a hundred such strange and fascinating points of interest.

NEW ORLEANS, LA.

1696 miles from New York.

No city in America remained for such a long period of years so distinctively foreign as New Orleans.

Clustering about its early life hang some of the most thrilling events in history, while all that bespeak the inimitable gallantry of the French, the passionate love and hatred born in the Spanish, and the strikingly brilliant race of Creoles, have given it a peculiarly individualized and original people, of whom Northerners know little or nothing and whom they find hard to approach ; but underneath burns the most hospitable courtesy, that trait for which the people of the South have justly received such renown.

SAN ANTONIO, TEX.

2267 miles from New York.

This city is one of the oldest in America. It is famous for its bright sunshine, clear atmosphere, and its old houses and streets.

One noted shrine is the Alamo, directly in the centre of the city. It was here that the renowned defense was made by Travis, Borne, Evans, and Davy Crockett with one hundred and forty-four men, against Santa Anna with fifteen hundred picked soldiers from the Mexican Army, who at last scaled the walls and butchered the starving besieged. The entire town had capitulated at promise of mercy and speedy release, but the word of Santa Anna was false and his nature treacherous. Four hundred and twelve prisoners, including the garrison, one Palm Sunday morning, were brought out in single file and shot down like dogs.

Government Hill, one of the finest military posts in America, should be visited ; it is easily reached, and abounds in interest.

EL PASO, TEX.

2891 miles from New York.

The quaintness of El Paso, with its picturesqueness of situation, is strongly marked. The city contains many new and handsome structures, including a county court house, schools, and churches.

LOS ANGELES, CAL.

3703 miles from New York.

As the Spanish so appropriately named it, "La Pueblo de la Reina de los Angeles" (town of the Queen of the Angels), so it deserves, for surely no more ideal spot for health, scenery, climate, and pleasure can well be imagined. It is situated on a slope of the Sierra Santa Monica, guarded and fortified against every possible chilling wind, in the midst of gardens, vineyards, and groves, yet as a city it has every convenience of transit and modern advanced improvements. Its residences present perfect pictures, surrounded as they are by parks, orange groves, and the most tempting walks. It is a magnificent centre, from which diverge innumerable spokes of interest. The city itself is undoubtedly destined to become the social metropolis of the Coast, for the climate must make it the choice spot for residence, and the business activity and railroad facilities are growing every year. Within a short distance by rail are the interesting towns of Anaheim, Santa Ana, San Pedro, Wilmington, Orange, and Westminster.

SAN DIEGO, CAL.

3326 miles from New York.

Historically, San Diego is the oldest California mission town on the southern sea coast, and was formerly situated some four miles north of its present location.

The Presidio, one-hundred-year-old palms, Padre Junipero's old mission, founded in 1769, and the mission of San Luis Rey near Oceanside, Mission Valley and Pala, abound in interest.

Several times a week one may invade Mexico by the train which runs around the peninsula to National City, the Sweet Water Reservoir, and Tia Juana. Tia Juana

owes allegiance to two republics, for the boundary line between Mexico and the United States runs through the town.
It presents a characteristic picture of shiftless Mexican life.

CORONADO BEACH, CAL.
Connected by ferry with San Diego.

On a narrow peninsula separating the waters of San
Diego Bay from the ocean is Coronado Beach, where the
mammoth Hotel Del Coronado stands, with the magnificent beach on one side and the blue waters of the bay on

HOTEL DEL CORONADO, SAN DIEGO.

the other. The hotel is palatial in finish, imposing in struct-
ure, and embodies every modern improvement, including a
complete electric lighting and steam heating plant. In its
gardens fruits from the tropic and temperate zones ripen side
by side, and the sweet odor from its artistically-designed
flower beds is a perfect lotion of refreshment. The tropical
court on the grounds is esteemed the most marvelous in the
country.

RIVERSIDE, CAL.

70 miles from Los Angeles.

Riverside is a perfect paradise of orange, fig, and almond groves. Its principal street, extending twelve miles in length and one hundred and thirty-two feet wide, is bordered along the entire distance with fruit, stately palm, and pepper trees. Plainly in view through the purity of the atmosphere the peaks of the San Bernardino range rise in majestic height a dozen miles away. The reclaiming of arid land by means of irrigation has been accomplished most comprehensively at Riverside, and the irrigating canals to be seen here are said to be the finest in the State. Here orange culture is scientifically pursued.

REDLANDS, CAL.

69 miles from Los Angeles.

A few miles eastward from San Bernardino, reveling, like its sister town, Riverside, in the midst of groves which have partly given the place its reputation, is the wealthy little town of Redlands, a centre of the seedless orange district. The situation of the place on the beautiful hills, over a thousand feet above the sea level, would have won for it, independent of the rich agricultural surroundings, a just reputation as a health resort.

PASADENA, CAL.

(CROWN OF THE VALLEY.)

10 miles from Los Angeles.

Like all of these originally Spanish settlements, Pasadena's history is interwoven with the romantic. It is really the nucleus around which clusters for miles in circuit the active growth of modern improvement on the moss-covered ruins of a past glory. At midwinter its gardens are all blooming, and its mild climate renders it a highly-favored resort for those in pursuit of health. The San Gabriel Valley, of which Pasadena is the crown, is about forty miles long and about ten wide, and at the extreme western portion, in a network of beautiful groves and vineyards, is Pasadena, covering an area of five miles, laid out with the most artistically-arranged gardens, drives, and walks. Southeast from the city is the largest winery in the world, and within comparatively short driving disance are the Sunny Slope and Baldwin Ranches. On the latter are some of the highest-bred horses in America.

ECHO MOUNTAIN HOUSE AND "YE ALPINE TAVERN," CAL.

The Echo Mountain House is situated on Mt. Lowe, thirty-five hundred feet above sea level, immediately overlooking the San Gabriel Valley, with mountains, foothills, ever verdant valleys, towns, old mission, islands, and ocean all in full view.

An additional attraction is the Lowe Observatory. It is temporarily located on Echo Mountain, and is reached by carriage drive from the hotel. Here also is located the great search light used at the Columbian Exposition, Chicago, the most powerful light in the world.

Four miles further up the mountain side, at an elevation of five thousand feet above sea level, is located "Ye Alpine Tavern," one thousand feet below the summit. This hotel was formally opened on December 14, 1895. It is reached from Echo Mountain House via an electric railway. Beyond the "Tavern" is Inspiration Point, which may be visited by carriage. From this point stretches out a magnificent panorama of the lower levels. The mountain slopes, furrowed by deep cañons, the winding rivers, cultivated fields and gardens, sweet cottages and opulent villas— all are clear and distinct from this immense height.

SANTA BARBARA, CAL.

110 miles north of Los Angeles.

This Nice of America, from a handful of people, almost all invalids from the East, has sprung into a resort whose climate and wonderful cures have been extolled in so high a key that its name is now known to almost every nation on the globe. It is directly on the coast, a little over one hundred miles north from Los Angeles, on a magnificent beach.

Its drives, pretentious homes and gardens are all attractive, while no small climatic credit is due to its sheltered position, screened by the high heads of the Santa Ynez Mountains, which rise in majestic grandeur at its back. The magnificent roads which radiate from the town invite equestrian exercise, which, with cycling, golfing, bathing and boating, are the principal diversions of the active people. Its gardens are famed for their prolific production of roses, no less than three hundred different varieties being cultivated in the town.

MONTEREY, CAL.

125 miles from San Francisco.

The old town of Monterey reposes in a shapely bend of the southern end of the Bay of Monterey.

A macadamized road known as the Eighteen-mile Drive, is without doubt the grandest drive on the continent. This road runs from the Hotel del Monte to Monterey, and there turns to the left and ascends a long hill of easy grade. The top is the crest of the ridge which runs out from the

HOTEL DEL MONTE, MONTEREY, CAL.

mainland, and when standing on the summit and looking away below a scene is pictured whose grandeur conquers description. It is the fairyland one might have imagined but never expected to witness. Down, down goes the road towards the bay, whose blue twinkling waters may be seen now and then through the road's border of oak and pine, sparkling like scattered gems. In and out of shady ravines leads the smooth drive, and after many windings of gently descending grade the bay is reached.

Continuing on the road, Pescadero Beach, Chinese Cove, and Pebble Beach are passed. The latter place has been famous for gathering pebbles, which many prize for the wonderful colors they possess. Right here at Monterey is the most curious and isolated species of cypress growth in the world. The bluffs are crowned with these strange trees, which cling to the rocks with fierce tenacity, their roots sprawling, clinging, grasping, seemingly with desperate strength, to the immovable crags which give them support. Nowhere else in the world is this species seen.

HOTEL DEL MONTE.

In the midst of the rank vegetation of the tropics and the magnificent old trees that gave shade to the zealous missionaries of old, is the Hotel del Monte. The entrance to this Eden is through avenues of massive and distorted live oaks and stately pines, which guard a palace where all in nature that calls forth exclamations of delight, all that charms and heals, has been harmonized by the high art improvements of the nineteenth century into an enchanting retreat of magnificence and comfort. The limit of money was not considered in its construction, and the brain service of artists and artisans of the highest order has been brought into requisition to give tone and feature to the embellishment of this fairy realm.

SANTA CRUZ, CAL.

80 miles from San Francisco.

The country around Santa Cruz is bold and imposing; one is carried through cañons and along the border of great yawning precipices, and a few miles beyond Santa Cruz the road passes through a grove of "mammoth trees," which go far to outrival those of the Mariposa Grove. A stop may be made to view the marvelous gigantic growth located at Big Trees Station. The location of Santa Cruz is delightful, embracing beautiful beaches and rocky bluffs, with a background of gardens and woods. The Lorenzo River wends its tortuous way through one side of the village and empties into the ocean close to the bathing ground. The Mission de la Santa Cruz, the twelfth of the twenty-one mission establishments founded by the Franciscan *padres* in 1791, and the origin of this present interesting and thriving place, is reached by a short walk.

SAN JOSÉ, CAL.

50 miles from San Francisco.

Fifty miles south from San Francisco, nestled in the heart of North Santa Clara's beautiful valley, is the enviable site of San José. Its very thoroughfares are orchards or vineyards, and the city one mammoth garden of great, varied, and warm beauty. One of the most delightful features of the San José visit is the ride over the Mt. Hamilton Stage Line route. This is accomplished in very commodious coaches, which leave in the morning and return in the afternoon, and the company has left nothing wanting to add to the greatest possible comfort of its guests.

Mt. Hamilton reaches an altitude of forty-two hundred and nine feet above the sea, and from its summit an indescribably grand view is obtained. It is surmounted by

one of the most completely-appointed observatories in the
world, founded by James Lick, the cost of which was close
to $1,000,000. Saturday evenings, between the hours of
seven and ten, visitors may look through the great tele-
scope, one of the largest in the world.

MENLO PARK, CAL.
(San Mateo County.)
32 miles from San Francisco.

A short and pleasant drive from Menlo Park Station is
the site at Palo Alto of the Stanford University, which
stands among the leading educational institutions of the
world. It was endowed by its founder, Hon. Leland Stanford, with $20,000,000, and is equipped with all the useful
paraphernalia which money can command or science in-
vent. The chairs are filled by the most eminent educators
in the land, and the curriculum is broad, liberal, and
comprehensive. The college is non-sectarian. A visit to
it and the famous Palo Alto stock farm, undoubtedly one
of the most extensive in the country, is productive of both
pleasure and profit.

SAN FRANCISCO, CAL.

At the time gold was discovered, only four hundred whites
comprised the population on the peninsula of San Francisco.
Directly in front of the site of the old Cliff House (de-
stroyed by fire in 1894), not three hundred yards out in the
ocean, are the rocky islets selected by hundreds of seals
for their sportive playground and homes. From here the
visitor can proceed about two hundred yards up the road
to the broad, white gateway of Mr. Adolph Sutro's handsome grounds, "Sutro Heights." Opposite the entrance
gate to the grounds the steam railway carries one back

again to the city along the water's edge, affording a
beautiful view of the Golden Gate, and also passes within
short distance of the Presidio Reservation, now the headquarters of the United States Military Department of the
Pacific; from here it runs to Central Avenue, where connection is made with the California Street cable cars, which

SEAL ROCKS, SAN FRANCISCO.

run every few minutes into the business centre of the city.
The private residences along California Street are noted
for their magnificence.

The most interesting quarter in all of San Francisco, the
one most talked about, and the equal of which cannot be

seen in any other city on the continent, is the Chinese quarter. The variety of occupations and the amount of business done by the Celestials is astonishing. A visit to the Chinese Joss house, where the idol sits enthroned in splendor, will prove interesting; but the most striking scene of all is to be found in the Chinese theatre.

SAN RAFAEL, CAL.

15 miles from San Francisco. Connected by ferry to Tiburon and rail to San Rafael. Via San Francisco and North Pacific Railways (Market Street). Via North Pacific Coast Company (Market Street) to San Rafael via Sausalito.

Within less than an hour's ride of the occidental metropolis, built at the foot of Mt. Tamalpais, in the midst of a diversified landscape of forest, valley, and glen, is San Rafael, the favorite abiding place for many of San Francisco's wealthy men, who have subdued the once wild growth into famous gardens and vineyards, and erected for miles along its broad avenues and drives costly mansions and artistic villas. Its peculiarly protected situation guards it from ocean fogs and chilly winds.

The detailed information above will give an idea of the easy mode of reaching it, and one visiting San Francisco should by all means include its suburb San Rafael.

SALT LAKE CITY, UTAH.

2705 miles from New York. 871 miles from San Francisco.

Salt Lake City is situated in the great Valley of the Jordan, west of the Wasatch Mountains, and just fifteen miles south of Great Salt Lake. The city is beautifully laid out, and possesses numerous attractive public buildings of note and worth. The streets are kept beautifully clean, especially in the residence portion, and there is an Oriental air about the city that carries one back to the banks of the biblical Jordan, and is unlike that of any other city in the Union. On Oil Creek, immediately where it emerges from the Range, are the grounds and offices of the Presidency of the Mormon Church. Separated from these by East Temple (Main) Street is Temple Block, conspicuous from the entire valley by reason of the turtle-roofed Tabernacle and white granite walls and towers of the Temple. On the same block are the Endowment House and Assembly Hall, both buildings connected with Mormon worship. The great Temple is of native gray granite, two hundred feet long, ninety feet wide, with towers two hundred and twenty feet high. It was begun in 1853, completed and dedicated in 1893, and cost $4,000,000. The Tabernacle is two hundred and fifty feet long, one hundred and fifty feet wide, and ninety feet high; seats thirteen thousand four hundred and fifty-six people; has the second largest organ in America, with three thousand pipes, and a well-trained choir of several hundred voices; service is held every Sunday at 2.00 P. M. Its acoustics are unequaled. Its roof is the largest wooden roof in the world unsupported by pillars. The Assembly Hall, in the same block, has a seating capacity of twenty-five hundred, and holds a very large pipe organ. The ceiling is elaborately decorated with scenes from prominent events in the history of the Mormon Church. Only one block away are the Bee Hive (the residence of the late Brigham Young), the Lion House, and the Gardo House, or Amelia Palace.

GLENWOOD SPRINGS, COL.

2325 miles from New York.

Glenwood Springs will be found to be one of the most interesting points visited. It is one of the great health resorts of the State, situated at the confluence of the Grand

River with the Roaring Fork, in a beautiful valley. Its altitude is about the same as that of Denver. It is especially noted for its hot sulphur springs, large out-door bathing pool and bath house, and hot vapor caves.

COLORADO SPRINGS, COL.

2033 miles from New York.

At Colorado Springs ample opportunity will be afforded to thoroughly view the charming city under the shadow of Pike's Peak, which heroic mount raises its snow-capped head like a cowled sentinel on guard over the treasured bit of garden earth below. The climate is grand, and the scenic attractions unrivaled. The place has won a marvelous reputation as a health resort. Seven miles away is the famous resort Manitou, with its world-renowned "Garden of the Gods," a park covering eight hundred acres, and surrounded on all sides by a rampart of hills. Within an hour's ride are the Cheyenne Cañons, Austin's Glen, Blair Athol, Queen's Cañon, and Glen Eyrie. No city on the continent, perhaps, is more picturesquely located or surrounded by more natural wonders. On all sides are seen signs of mighty upheavals and the action of ages.

DENVER, COL.

1958 miles from New York.

During the mad rush of '58 a gold camp was pitched at the junction of Cherry Creek and the Platte and christened Auraria. From this small beginning sprang Denver, the pushing, bright, and cultured city of the plain, the social and commercial centre not only of Colorado, but of the entire middle West. Within a figurative stone's throw of its walls are the world-known cattle ranches and silver-producing sections. From its heights may be seen in all their indescribable grandeur the snow-capped peaks of the Rockies, Long's Peak a short distance to the north, and far away to the south the dim outline of Pike's Peak. The industry of wresting the precious metals from their rocky prisons is here carried on upon a very extensive scale and may be seen a short distance outside of the city. To the returning traveler Denver is the portal to the populous East.

CHICAGO, ILL.

912 miles from New York.

The proud city of Chicago, the seat of the greatest of the world's expositions, is entirely too large a subject for anything like an adequate description in these limited pages. In fact, anything more than a mere mention would be superfluous, as millions already are acquainted with the exhibition of characteristic American ingenuity displayed there on all sides. For financial worth and commercial standing it outranks every other city in the country, with the exception of New York. Its situation on the great lakes and in the very centre of a perfect network of railroads indisputably foreshadows even a brighter future. The indefatigable push and rush of the people are seen here as nowhere else in the United States, nor in the world might be truthfully added, and a casual inspection of its immense buildings and nineteenth century ideas will be nothing less than a revelation to those unfamiliar with its unparalleled growth and wonderful prosperity.

The park system is very elaborate, and includes about two thousand acres. Lincoln Park is on the north side, about two miles distant; Douglas and Central Parks on the west side, about four miles ; and the South Parks, in the south part of the city, between six and seven miles. The chief approaches to the latter are through the Grand and Drexel Boulevards. Jackson and Washington Parks, where the Columbian Exposition was held, an international affair of so great an importance to the world at large that a fame for Chicago has been perpetuated which will live forever, may be reached either by the Illinois Central Railroad, suburban trains, or by one of the elevated railways. The river is crossed by thirty-five swinging bridges, and there are also two tunnels, at Washington and La Salle Streets. The Union Stock Yards are in the southern part of the city. They cover three hundred and fifty acres, and are the most extensive in the world.

TOURS TO JACKSONVILLE, FLA.

A series of tours from New England, New York, Philadelphia, Baltimore, Washington, and other principal points
on the Pennsylvania System will be run, leaving New York
January 24, February 7 and 21, and March 7, 1899.

The tours will admit of a visit of TWO ENTIRE WEEKS
in the Flowery State.

Tickets for the last tour will be valid for return by regular
trains until May 31, 1899.

The period allowed is amply sufficient to admit of a
thorough tour of all the interesting places in the Peninsula.

Passengers from New England will join the special train
at New York or Philadelphia.

Rates for the round trip, $65.00 from Boston, $50.00 from
New York, $48.00 from Philadelphia, and proportionate
rates from other stations.

TOURS, NEW YORK TO WASHINGTON, D. C.

DECEMBER 27, 1898,
JANUARY 19, FEBRUARY 16,
MARCH 9 and 28, APRIL 20,
MAY 11, 1899,

are the dates selected for the winter and spring tours
to Washington, D. C., under the popular personally-conducted system of the Pennsylvania Railroad Company.
Tickets will be sold at rate of $14.50 from New York and
$11.50 from Philadelphia, including accommodations at
the leading hotels of the Capital in addition to round-trip
transportation.

TOURS TO OLD POINT COMFORT, RICHMOND, AND WASHINGTON.

Will leave New York and Philadelphia

DECEMBER 27, 1898,
JANUARY 28,
FEBRUARY 25,
MARCH 18,
APRIL 1, 15, and 29, 1899.

Round-trip tickets for these tours, including transportation in each direction, box luncheon going, and one and three-fourths days' board at Old Point Comfort, and valid to return on regular trains via Cape Charles Route within six days, will be sold at rate of $15.00 from New York, $12.50 from Philadelphia, and proportionate rates from other points.

Tickets for these tours to Old Point Comfort and Richmond, and return via Washington, including all necessary expenses for the entire trip of six days, will be also sold at rate of $34.00 from New York and $31.00 from Philadelphia.

For detailed itineraries and full information regarding any of these tours apply to ticket agents; Tourist Agent, 1196 Broadway, New York; 860 Fulton Street, Brooklyn; Thomas Purdy, Passenger Agent Long Branch District, Newark, N. J.; B. Courlaender, Jr., Passenger Agent Baltimore District, Baltimore, Md.; C. Studds, Passenger Agent Southeastern District, Washington, D. C.; Thos. E. Watt, Passenger Agent, Western District, Pittsburg, Pa., or address

GEO. W. BOYD,
Assistant General Passenger Agent,
Broad Street Station, Philadelphia.

TOURS, BOSTON TO WASHINGTON, D. C.

Six-day personally-conducted tours to Washington, D. C.,
will leave Boston

DECEMBER 26, 1898,
JANUARY 23,
FEBRUARY 6 and 27,
MARCH 13 and 27,
APRIL 3, 10, and 24, 1899.

Tickets, including meals *en route* (except on Fall River
Line Steamer returning), side trip to Mt. Vernon, and board
at Washington's leading hotels, will be sold at rate of $23.00
from Boston.

Tickets and all information pertaining to the tours from
Boston may be obtained of D. N. Bell, Tourist Agent,
Pennsylvania Railroad Company, 205 Washington Street,
Boston, or

GEO. W. BOYD,
Assistant General Passenger Agent,
Broad Street Station Philadelphia.

www.ingramcontent.com/pod-product-compliance
Lightning Source LLC
Chambersburg PA
CBHW021438090426
42739CB00009B/1528